The Financial Piggy weekly

Feti$h Magazine for financial submi$$ives

Issue #6 September 19th 2012

By

Goddess Bella Donna

The topics and content of this Magazine are for mature adults (18 years and older) interested in fetish and BDSM. They are not intended for anyone under the age of 18 or to those individuals offended by topics of such nature. Purchasing this magazine as a minor or purchasing this magazine for a minor is against the law, please respect this.

Opinions in this Magazine are those of the individual writers and do not necessarily reflect the opinions of the fetish / BDSM community at large.

Published September 2012
Publication Company: LULU Inc.

ISBN #: 978-1-300-21285-0

Content:

Piggy fiction Story and draining command Part 3

That wasn't so hard piggy, was it? Fondly ruffles your hair. See you are learning already and if you were a good little piggy you have already accumulated a few piggy points on your report card.

Oh dear me, I forgot to explain about piggy points didn't I? Well Goddess was so busy training you little pets already that it just slipped my mind. Piggy points are assigned each time you didn't just move on to the next section, but actually filled the commands as you should have. For each command you filled well and in full you receive 2 piggy points from me. At the end of camp you can trade your piggy points in for a reward. You will have the option to buy the rewards chart for $5.00 for one additional piggy point so you can choose what reward you would like that fits your accumulated piggy points. You get bonus piggy points if you go above and beyond the draining commands I make. So if you send $50 instead of $30 for example you have just earned yourself a few additional piggy points. How many I won't tell you, but trust me you want to gain as many piggy points as you can. For each half done command (you forget to write the note exactly as outlined etc) I take one piggy point away. So make sure you do it correctly.

Now that this is out of the way let's move on.

It is meal time now and piggies do need to eat. Remember you are no longer allowed to eat like human being but need to eat out of your piggy bowls with your hands behind your back. As I lead you to your feeding station you will see a bowl filled with macaroni and cheese, cut up steak, and your favorite vegetable mixed in. In the drinking bowl you find fresh cold clean water. (Prepare this meal just as described now and set it up in the bowls to eat and drink! I want a photo of you eating the meal piggy style and a photo of the prepared bowls. Send them both to me at http://www.niteflirt.com/mysteria with a $10.00 tribute... In the note you must write… Thank you for teaching me how to eat properly as a cash pet!)

I sit on my special Mistress Chair and enjoy a similar meal eating it from a fine china plate and drinking a glass of delicious chilled red wine while watching my little piggy students snuffling up their meals. I smile spreads over my face at your dirty little faces and ever so often I can't help but laugh out loud at a particularly eager little piggy. Your face turns red and your cock stiffens inside its cage when you hear my laughter. What you don't realize yet is that I have added a little bit of Viagra to the food all nice and crushed up which should be taken affect here shortly.

The meal time is over and the Viagra has already started taking affect. You are getting hornier by the minute and your cock is straining uncontrollably in its cage. You are so desperate that you even hump the air. If you touch your cock or attempt to touch your cock or balls I will zap you with the electricity boy.

Come with me piggy I command and start walking you to the exercise arena. There I am pairing you up 2 at a time and you will have to race down a 100 yard stretch on your hands and knees. A couple of gimps who I keep around just for the races will assist me here. One each is behind the little piggy racers and will drive his or her piggy on with well-aimed hits of a crop to the piggies ass. Trust me they will do their best because the loser of the piggy race will not only be in trouble himself but his gimp will be as well. The gimp has to suffer through 1000 lashes of my heaviest 20 strand latigo leather flogger I have. Not a nice feeling I assure you. So yes they will do their best.

Now of course there is a lot more than just crawling really fast to win the race. There are several tribute stations set up throughout the 100 yard stretch. You have to make your tribute quickly and precise before you can move further. Your gimp will give you medium blows to your ass with the crop while you make the tribute in order to remind you to go fast.

You need to register yourself in for the first race now. Failure to register in and race will result in an automatic $100 penalty which you will be send via paytoview to your account and you will not be allowed to continue on until you pay this fine. So don't skip this step.

Send a $10.00 tribute to http://www.niteflirt.com/mysteria now and with it put your piggy identification number and write starting the race now Goddess.

As soon as both of the competitors are registered in race begins and the winner will be rewarded with 15 additional piggy points while the loser will be send a $25.00 loser penalty paytoview and lose 10 piggy points. So you want to make sure you win. This race is timed and I am keeping an eye on the clock to see how quickly your tributes are coming in.

You start racing and after 1 minutes of crawling you come to the next tribute station. At the station you find this note: Log into your Amazon.com account and send me a $20.00 Amazon.com E-Certificate to GoddessBellaDonna@cox.net in the "from" put your piggy identification number and in the text body put racestop 1 Goddess. Do it as quickly as you can, remember the race doesn't continue until you have it completed. The race continues in a minute in the next part.

Making a first tribute that is pleasing

The first tribute seems to be one of the hardest "issues" for most people on both sides of the financial domination or fetish fence to overcome. If you, as a submissive, want to make a good impression on the Lady whose attention you are trying to gain, it is always a good idea to stand out from among the boys who are attempting the exact same thing.

As Money Mistresses and Fetish Queens we often deal with hundreds of people who try to get our attention for a wide variety of reasons. Every one of those guys have the same Agenda you do (getting time, conversation, attention, their fetish desires met) but often come out of different motivation to one another. Now on the outside looking in (the way we see you) most of you start out the exact same way and to be painfully honest unless you do something wonderful to be worth remembering you'll fade away in our minds rather quickly.

What makes a man stand out among hundreds of other men seeking our attention?

The rare skill of showing actual interest in us beyond our looks, your fetish desires and us being a means to an end of getting yourself off! With other words you interest in us as the living breathing woman who happens to be a Domina as well. Having an interest is very important as well in helping you discover what the perfect initial tribute would be short of being told and it being made an order. Remember you want to stick out, not just be one of the masses, so if you can actually discern what would please her the most and then make that your initial tribute you will most certainly be remembered for your earnestness in wanting to please her.

The rare skill of listening. I know you think you are listening (or reading) what she has to say, but most of you guys only listen to part of what is being said most of the time. For a lot of men have a short attention span and spot listening or reading is a serious problem. It is usually one of the top five reasons why they end up getting disciplined or punished when and if they do manage to find a Lady to serve. It is also one of the reasons women do the one thing you all hate so much – nag you! Nagging being the constant repeating of topic and the same thing being said in a dozen different ways! We do this because you "don't listen CORRECTLY". Meaning you get bored or sidetracked and shut off part of your listening skills half way through. This results in you not "knowing" everything you need know or should know, us getting frustrated by your lack of follow through and attention, and you getting annoyed because we are going to do this again in a day or two.

Now that might work just fine with your wife, girlfriend or mommy, but it most certainly won't work with your Mistress without some serious consequences in the long run. So if the rare skill of listening correctly can safe your ass later, it most certainly is a great skill in helping you finding out what she would enjoy the most at that point and time.

So now we have listening correctly and paying attention during a conversation with the Lady you are interested in.

Being willing to go the extra mile and putting HER first.

95% of guys actually willing to move forward and make their initial tribute stay focused on what they want to give rather than what she really would like to have.

Most gifts given are either sexy clothing, fetish oriented items, or something the guy finds hot. At that point it stops being about her and still is just about you and what you want.

I call those "stroke off gifts" and that is exactly what they are. Something you can stroke off to thinking about.

A boy who wants to make the Lady happy and a great first impression as a potential financial slave won't do that.

He will have already paid attention, listened and is now ready to give to her in the ways she desires to be contributed to.

Cash is probably the number 1 favorite gift of most Ladies because they can spend it any way and anywhere they decide to. Now of course you are going to be in a "how much" dilemma.

I can't tell you for every Lady what is acceptable but I can give you a general idea of how I see it.

A base minimum first tribute should be $50 to $100. Anything under that really is a bit of an insult. If you can't even afford $50 you shouldn't be asking to become her cash slave.

An average first tribute is between $100 to $200. It shows you aren't cheap and you appreciate the time she is taking with you and the attention she is / has given to you.

You want to really impress her, go $250 and up for a first tribute.

Now if you want to make me really take notice you split is apart a little bit. You do the majority in a cash tribute, but you buy one thing off my top Wishlist as well that I have mentioned either in conversation or on my blog. This will show me that you are willing to go the extra mile to make me happy. You are giving me the cash so I can use it for anything I desire, but you have also paid enough attention and listened closely enough to pick out ONE GIFT ITEM I really had my heart set on.

Doing more than the bare bones minimum (both in the material sense and in the effort sense) always sticks out, since most people by nature can't be bothered with that.

Remember what a tribute really is. A tribute is a gift of devotion, appreciation, respect and adoration given to someone you see as standing above you. If you wish to serve the Lady as your Domina or Goddess then this should automatically apply. She should, in your mind at least, stand above you or be superior to you. When you give your tribute or gift of devotion out of that mindset it becomes a lot easier to want to please her. It becomes automatically important that you go the extra mile in choosing just the perfect gift to give to her to set you apart.

Most Ladies will let you know what they want or what the minimum is they will accept from you. So it isn't as if you aren't getting any help once she demands a show of sincerity as it is often termed. If you want to stand out so, really want to be noticed by her and have a jump up on the other guys so to speak, you don't want to wait until she makes a demand. You want to do it before that point.

Now a last bit of advice. If you are sending an initial tribute with your slave application or request to speak to her but have never spoken to her before, the minimum ($50 - $100) is perfectly fine.

If however you have already had the pleasure of her company and conversation you should really look at more the average to impressive.

There is nothing as wonderful for us Ladies as receiving a gift we didn't have to push you for demand first. Sure being greedy and demanding is a lot of fun when we play with our toys (established to us boys or our personal slaves), but in the very beginning it is a lot nicer when we see you doing it out of adoration and respect.

I'll leave you with the mental image of a suitor on his knees before a powerful Lady, his head bowed in humility and holding up gifts to her. That should be you my dear boys!

8 Ideas to serve a Lady on a small budget

Some of you guys really want to serve someone special but your money is horribly tight and you can't afford to make higher financial contributions to please her.

That doesn't mean so that you can just get her attention for nothing and yes even those of you who are extremely tight should be able to give at least something financially to her. During my mentorship classes for new to the fetish Money Mistresses the question of what is the bare bones minimum that should be acceptable from a slave comes up frequently and how much time should he receive from the Lady in return.

As to the time there is no clear cut answer since our styles are so vastly different and the amusement level of the guys are too. As for an amount however I advise them to never accept less than $25.00 a week and that MUST be supplemented by work service they provide.

In all reality if a full grown man can't even make enough money to have $25.00 in play money or pocket money (which is what you should be spending your tributes out off) he needs to be out there looking for a better job or a second job rather than trying to play around on the internet and on fetish sites. He is dangerously close to losing everything he has. In my opinion, when it comes to that point, we owe it to them to just send them away and ignore them for their own good.

Now I mentioned work service to supplement this little bit of cash and this is where you boys usually start getting confused or want to bark like little yippy puppies. If you want to have a place at her feet and get her attention you need to carry your weight somehow and no loves showing her your cock and stroking off is not a gift to her.

So here are 10 things you can do that will serve HER well and that will show you are at least trying to be worthwhile.

#1 Become her social media marketing puppet!
You boys spend so much time browsing around on the internet, participating in Twitter Chat, socialize on Facebook, and often give your opinions on my different fetish communities. By doing this you are already well equipped to market or advertise for her. Put her link into your signature. Talk about your adoration for her and add a link to her. With other words help other boys find out about her and maybe have new little cash pets crawl to her feet due to your efforts.

#2 Research for her!

As a Domina we are constantly learning new things. We are forever trying to improve our toy bags, our websites, our xyz. What we don't have a lot off most of the time is sitting down and really research things. So why don't you take that very time consuming task of her hands. Ask her to assign you a few research projects she needs done a week and you go out and do them for her. Make sure you keep a detailed logged of what you find and where. Compile it into a short list and give the links for references. With other words you become her personal research assistant.

#3 Get crafty!
Not every one of you boys can do this because some of you are just as unskilled as they come, but if you do have the tools and the knowhow of leather crafting and wood working put those skills to use. Make some toys and tools for her play bag. Floggers, paddles, harnesses, cuffs, collars etc are not that difficult to make. When you make them yourself they cost the fraction of the price you would pay in the big fetish stores. So instead of paying $99 and up for a twenty strand flogger or mediocre quality, you can make if for roughly $30 with a lot higher quality once you learn how to. Not only that, but once you get really good at it, you might just have a sideline for income.

#4 Learn or use your real time service skills

What are some things you can do around the house or by hand which actually is worth something? Since you are long distance most of the time you can't clean her house for her, take out the trash etc. But can you fix shoes? Can you sew? Are you good at repairing cameras? Do you see where I am going with this?

#5 Get a small side job and give the money to her!

Deliver some newspapers before work. Do some handiwork around the neighborhood. Rent yourself out as a furniture mover. Little odd and end jobs when you can get them (of course you have to actually look for them too) can be a good source of a little bit of additional income for you. Now it becomes a lovely show of your desire to do better for your Mistress when you give additional money which you had to work extra for.

#6 Earn some points and trade them in for gift cards for her!

Places like Swagbucks, PointsandPrizes, Superpoints etc allows you to earn points by just clicking buttons, watching some ads, playing online games etc. You can redeem the points when you have accumulated enough for Gift Cards which you can give to your Lady. If she happens to be part of the same website sign on under her and earn points plus give her the referral bonus.

#7 Sign up on a phone sex site and become an operator!

Great for sissy gurls and bi guys. You want to be nasty and dirty so much so earn some money with your dirty imagination. Take some phone calls, do some webcam sessions and have the money you earn go into your Mistress account.

#8 Topsites, Directories and PR

Find topsites, adult directories and Press Release places that allow adult content. Add your Mistress site to them and send her the snippets of code that need to be added on her site. If she trusts you enough you can add them yourself. If she films, write Press Releases for each of her new clips and send them to the correct PR places. Loads of work most of us just don't find the time for.

The most important thing is that you don't just promise you'll do it, but you really have to be willing to do the work and do a good job at it. Keep logs of your work always and have it presentable to her whenever she decides to ask for it.

Work on it every day for at least an hour or two. Stay focused on your work for her. You are now more than ever a slave since you are giving to her out of your wallet and are actually putting effort into serving her in your "free time".

Just remember that when you do make yourself obligated as a slave to undertake one of those options and you decide to grow lazy on doing it, you will quickly become worthless in all aspects. The time you receive from her isn't for the little money amount you send alone, you have to sweat for it too.

Findom Interview: Miss KeeKee

Findoms, findoms everwhere and the styles? As different as night and day that is for certain. Now for those of you who are not familiar with this section of the Magazine yet let me explain it to you real fast.

I belong to several different communities and over the years I have watched, read and often interacted with a lot of different Ladies. Both fetish Queens as well as Financial Mistresses. From old school to new age styles. From young to well older like myself. Some are very new to the fetish, while others are very experienced Ladies with a longstanding domination history to their name. Some of them are pure Dominas, while others are Switches. Some are Fetish based Ladies (fetish Queens) while others are domination based Ladies (financial Mistresses). The variety is endless. There have been many Ladies who have stood out over the years to me.

Some of these Ladies share very similar philosophies to mine, while others are the complete opposite of me. The one thing they have in common is that they are all wonderful Ladies and deserve to be worshipped and served well in their own right. I feel proud to consider them my fellow Ladies / peers and in some cases even my dear friends.

It is my mission via these Findom Interviews to introduce you over time to some amazing Ladies who I couldn't help but notice and have watched for some time. I want to showcase a wide variety of different styles, age groups, ethnicity and philosophies to you in the hope that you will find the Lady of your dreams among them.

This week I would like to continue my Findom Interviews by introducing you to the lovely Miss KeeKee. A very creative Lady with a spark and a joy de vivre which will wrap you right around her little finger! This young Lady knows exactly what she wants and has some very cool dreams for her future. She is very gracious but she doesn't pull punches and you will always know where you stand with her. Now enough of the intro from me…

What is the name you go by as a Domina or Fetish Queen?

I go by a variation of names on different sites. They are Miss KeeKee, Mystress Ciarah and Keyairah

How did you come up with that name and does it have any particular meaning to you?

KeeKee is short for Cairah/Keyairah which is Gaelis for little dark one, My brother gave Me this nick name and it is very special to Me.

When is your date of birth (for the boys to spoil you on that special day):

February 25th 1983. I am a Pisces

Do you consider yourself a Financial Mistress or a Fetish Queen?

I am a Financial Mistress

How long have you been an active findom now (both real time and online) and how did you get your start in it?

I have been active for roughly 15 years. I started out as a paid "Mommy" in high school.

What do you find to be the most important aspects of financial domination and financial fetish? Are the one and the same to you or do you separate them?

I like the control I have when, well controlling a boys finances. It is the ultimate control, and can be done on longer terms. Financial fetish is a shorter term and doesn't give the same control as Financial Domination. Yes I do separate the two.

What are you looking for in your boys?

Loyalty, Honesty, Obedience, and of course Submission

Do you mind telling us a little bit about you the woman behind the Title?

I am a naturally dominant woman. I enjoy the outdoors,sports and cars. I am a Wiccan Priestess. I have a family whom I am very close with. I love the holidays. I have a regular job outside of findom.

What are some of your goals in life?

I'd like to own My own nail salon and eventually when I retire I want to own/operate a bed & breakfast in New Jersey.

Do you have one particular big dream you are working on achieving?

Next year I will be going back to school to become a nail technician. This will help with My goal of owning My own nail salon.

If any of my Readers would be interested in contacting you to see if he can be of service to you, how would he go about it and which steps must he follow to do it right?

They may contact Me on any of the sites I've given here. They must follow My rules, found here:

http://www.findoms.com/MyztressKeyairah/blog/proper-approach-my-rules/

Do you do any Adult Industry related things? (clips4sale, kinkbomb, Niteflirt etc?)If yes can we get your links and can you tell us a little about them and what you do there?

Niteflirt :

http://www.niteflirt.com/listings/show/9805553-Smokin-Hot-Mistress

http://www.niteflirt.com/listings/show/9825543-Miss-KeeKee-Smoking-for-you

Is there anything else you would like to share with us? Any thoughts, things you feel the boys should know?

My favorite colors are black and pink. I dress goth.

Please give us your website or blog URL and any way of contacting you that you allow boys to have.

http://www.findoms.com/MyztressKeyairah/

https://fetlife.com/users/1610819

http://misskeekeesblog.blogspot.com/

http://sweetnessmanipulates.blogspot.com/2012/08/this-story-is-told-in-my-soft-husky.html

http://misskeekeesblog.blogspot.com/2012/07/practice-erotica.html

Well there you have it boys! Go visit her blogs and get to know her even better. Personally I love the dream of her very own Nail Salon, as well as Bed & Breakfast. You boys should really contribute financially towards making it happen!

A journey Part 1 by Victor (owned slave recount)

Is seeing the different styles and Ladies is important to give you a good idea of what is out there, then hearing the voices and recounts of fetish boys, subs, and slaves is important to showcase to you that you are not alone in your confusion and often "twisted" journeys to the goal.

All the gentlemen you will see featured in the "slave voices" are slaves, subs, or fetish boys who stood out to me for some special reason. Most of those aren't my slaves or serving boys, but are owned by another Lady, serve as community "whores", or a free spirited fetish boys with an interesting story to tell. I do this on purpose since I don't want to "just advertise" for myself. Ever so often I'll ask some of my boys to share, but in most cases it will be boys I have nothing to do with.

I am what you would consider a "Watcher" and that means I sit back and watch the behavior, responses, wordings, demeanor etc of different boys I see in open forums, communities etc. Not every submissive is the same, just like not every Domina is the same. For some of them being a slave comes easy, while for others it is a bit of a tougher road. Some of them are feisty and opinionated but always honest and honorable. Some of them are almost puppy like in their devotion to their Mistress, while others have a bit of a bite to them.

What all of you have in common is that it was a Journey in self discovery with often some bumps and bruises along the way. Self doubt, confusion, anxiety, and a void to be filled.

This week I am proud to be able to introduce Victor to you. He is the owned slave of the lovely Miss Deviant Bitch, a Lady I have known for many years now from various communities. When I approached Deviant about "loaning her boy to me for this article task" she told me that she was ok with it, but that he was a boy of his own mind. Not something that surprised me to be honest, because it was just this very open and outspoken attitude in many blog post responses which I had read that had gotten my attention and made me want to hear and post his story for you to learn something from. He is a fine example of an outspoken strong willed gentleman who will bend his knee to ONLY the Lady whom he sees as VERY SPECIAL. He is always very polite, but he is nobody's fool.

Victor informed me that his story could easily be a book and I told him well how about writing it in 3 parts than. This is the first of those parts and I think it is going to be quiet the journey by the time he is done recounting it for us.

Thank you Victor from the bottom of my heart for the courage and honesty it takes to make yourself this vulnerable to strangers!

…and now ….

A JOURNEY – CHAPTER I

Hello. My name is Victor. I am 42 years old. I am from the UK … only one of these statements is true, I leave you decide which.

I have reasons for wearing a cloak of anonymity, but there is only one person who I have told the reasons why. Others will know of course, and they will feature in this narrative if they have journeyed with me, others may guess if our paths have ever crossed. For those that wonder … yes, this is a cautionary tale, take heed.

I have been asked by the Goddess Bella Donna to submit this article for inclusion in her publication, so if you are reading this then my submission has been approved! My brief has been simple, to put down in words my experiences in leading up to this point in my servitude, and my journey towards my now being owned. And at all times to be wholly honest. A simple brief, but not a simple task by any means!

So, other than two parts from three of my opening paragraph, the remainder here is an entirely true and honest account to the best of my abilities. Names may have been changed to protect the innocent!

I am now owned by a wonderful Lady going by the online name of Deviant Bitch … which is strange because actually she is neither. She is a person of intense passion and humanity, gloriously sexual and sharp as a tack, funny and sad all at the same time. Yes she is WOMAN, and I have never felt happier or safer now that she has embraced me into her arms and into her world. I can tell her anything and she knows everything.

I was born into this world the eldest son of a priest. At the age of 12 I was sent away to an English boarding school, and yes some of the rumours are true! For the next 5 years and all through my adolescence I grew up apart from my parents and my family, my innocence exposed and a soul infinitely corruptible. Porn material abounded, and I found myself masturbating constantly to images and fantasies of dominant and superior women, reading and absorbing stories of increasing depravity about men who became their slaves and servants, and cumming again and again and again to those fantasies. Fantasies?

I left school at 17, I didn't want to go to university I had had enough of the education system thanks very much! I needed to work, to earn money, to get out and explore the world. Initially I went home, but I didn't belong there of course! Nevertheless, I first had to find a job and earn money, a church family doesn't have money, and of course work was in the city and there I began to commute to work an hour each way, surrounded on packed trains by more gorgeous women than I knew existed, all of course looking down their nose at this pimply youth daring to share their space! I had just turned 18 with all my hormones raging, and I was sitting on the train watching these fabulous women, every day, there and back, lusting like crazy but never daring approach. And hoping they would notice the pound notes I would "carelessly" leave peeking from my coat pockets … what the FUCK was all that about?? More fantasy? Starting to edge reality …

I left home after a couple of years, 20 and still a virgin, and still wanking furiously over my fantasy women. Suitcases full of my burgeoning porn collection … Sadie Stern Monthly, Janus, She Who Must Be Obeyed, etc etc. But this was my secret, to the world I wore a mask, Mr Normal. I got with a girlfriend, I partied, I worked, I played, and yes I lost my virginity! Everything was great … wasn't it? I finished with that girlfriend (damn I still regret that but I couldn't do it I just couldn't, didn't know why, do now), found another, and another, and another … never more than one at a time I was loyal see. Then I got married, a home maker, go figure!

Happy now? No. Well maybe for 6 months, then oh shit I think I made a mistake. Did I tell her, did I tell anyone, about my fantasies? Of course not. And I started going to see "ladies" … not for sex, oh no I don't cheat, this was for chastisement. But fuck it turned me on, it became an addiction and, of course, it COST … money, more and more money!

The marriage lasted 15 years, hey, church dude, we don't do divorce here! We had a son, he's grown now, I love him more than my own life. She and me are still friendly, we did our best but of course I couldn't hack it in the end, I was starting to hanker more and more for that elusive goal, the goal I hadn't quite got my head around yet, hadn't quite yet homed in on and brought into sharp focus. Tease? Jeepers tell me about it! Denial? FUCK YES!! Don't talk to me about tease and denial, it's been my lifestyle!

And all the time working my butt off to earn the money, the money I needed to keep my family, and the money I needed to feed my addiction. Tied spread-eagled across a bed, pinioned across a bench, strapped to a frame, even suspended or just over the knee. Ass cheeks glowing, sometimes striped sometimes bruised but careful, have to be discreet … and always ALWAYS my wallet stuffed full of cash and lying open on the dresser. And the internet wasn't even invented yet …

To be continued

Project Duke
A service opportunity!

Hello little puppet, you are going to serve my little mini-van as his restorations bitch. With other words you are going to go out suck cock, get fucked up the ass, and try to find as many Sissy Slut housekeeping jobs for perverted old men as you can to pay for the cost of my mini-van being fully restored and set up the way I desire.

You see I have a big heart for aging things and love keeping those who have served me loyally for many years around. Duke, my little blue mini-van, falls under that and maybe if you can prove yourself over time so will you.

Now let's get started on what you need to do to get things moving in the right direction, meaning you debasing yourself in the most delightful and nasty way in order to make money for ME.

Let's start with getting really down and dirty, as in actually crawling around on your poor little hands and knees with your panty glad tushy up in the air. Cleaning some dirty lonely old man's kitchen or living room. Make sure you wear your best maids uniform for this. Do a good job cleaning but give him a good show as well. You know there is nothing as dirty as making a sad old man so horny that he would be willing to pay a little sissy bitch like you to clean another set of pipes as well.

So how do you find those jobs? Easy first of all you need to dress yourself up in your maids uniform, nice wig and make up on. High heels and stockings. You know the whole nine yards. Take a photo of yourself cleaning the Kitchen, scrubbing your floor on your hands and knees, and vacuuming or dusting. Take those 3 very industrious photos and add them to a Craigslist ad you are going to create. Make it clear in your ad that you are a Sissy Gurl so you don't run into the risk of getting your ass kicked by someone who doesn't find it amusing.

You will charge $20.00 an hour you CLEAN as in actually cleaning. Give a list of sissy housekeeping services you offer. Dishes, window cleaning, dusting, vacuuming, laundry etc. You get my meaning.

Out of every $20 you make you may keep $5.00 for new sissy clothing, but the other $15.00 go to me. You will report in detail how many yours you have cleaned, for whom and what you had to clean.

Cock Sucking – Sucking cock is not about you enjoying it my little whore, but about you making sure your stud enjoys it. Which means you will do a damn good job of it. Don't take less than $50 for every cock you suck bitch. You are allowed to keep $15.00 out of this and the other $35.00 goes to me. Again I want a full report. Don't forget to lick those sweaty balls while you are at it.

Getting fucked – oh now I know you are all excited about getting your slutty little boy pussy slammed into by a big hard cock. I bet this will become your favorite activity soon and of course you will whimper ever so nicely while you are getting fucked harder and harder. Don't forget to lick his ass nicely first to really get his prostrate working. Nice slow swipes with your tongue at first and once you see his balls filling up nicely, you start probing your tongue into his asshole. When his cock is as hard as a ramrod you crawl in front of him like a good little sissy whore and beg him nicely to fuck you like the slut bitch you are. Do you think your pussy is worth $75.00? If not you better get there. You may keep $25.00 of this for your new sissy clothing, the other $50 are mine.

Every week until your new mechanical Master has been repaired fully and to my satisfaction you will be given an amount you need to earn during this week. Now that amount is the money you will be handing over to me not the money you will be making.

Fail to make the cash because you couldn't whore your ass out that week or didn't find generous enough Sissy Tricks you will pay it out of your own pocket.

Now let's begin with the goal for this week and I'll make it a simple one.

Master Duke needs a full oil-change and I want his breaks fully replaced. Now your goal for this week is $250.00.

That shouldn't be too hard for you. Only 5 times getting your ass fucked, or up to 10 of the other sissy service you provide. Get to it restoration bitch!

Send the money once it is earned to me either via Greendot MoneyPack Refills (USA) to GoddessBellaDonna@cox.net, or via Niteflirt Tribute (http://www.niteflirt.com/mysteria) for all others.

Don't be tardy my little Bitches, you wouldn't want me to have to really punish you, would you?

Oh and for the extremely inquisitive gurls among you who just always have to ask another question before working, you can get on your knees and call me at: **1-800-863-5478 ext: 9473405 (You will be charged by the minute)**

Let's test your "paying attention skills"

A task!

I collect a few TV series and one I am only missing a few more Episodes from. The series I am looking for has a mechanical dog in it, several companions, and has been around for a long time.

Now I am looking for the name of the Series and the name of the Actor who played my favorite reincarnation of the main Character.

Get it correct and you will be permitted to give yourself 200 strokes (masturbation), get is wrong and you will have to kneel on rice for 10 minutes and give yourself 100 swats with a belt on the ass.

Send your answer to me at goddessbelladonna@cox.net

To make it even more interesting, this particular character reincarnation always carries 2 items with him. Not a clothing article. What are they?

I want you to add the 2 items into this sentence.

"I am (enter name of character) and I would love to give xyz and xyz to Goddess Bella Donna as a gift."

Write the correctly filled out sentence 100 times. Handwriting boys no copy and paste BS.

Send it to me scanned in to goddessbelladonna@cox.net

Don't forget to make your financial contribution towards my vacation soon. *winks*

(http://www.niteflirt.com/mysteria)

easiest for all to make a cash tribute.

Grocery Cash Piggy and Forced Feeding Slave!

It pleases me to combine two different fetishes I deeply enjoy into one lovely task and possible position for you. I love to fatten my piggies up via my forced eating and forced weight gain instructions, essentially turning them into the gluttonous human food dump that they secretly fantasize about being and transforming them from fit often reasonably sexually active and decent looking men into fat, man breast spouting, sexually inept and cucked forced feminized boys. That of course it the first of the two fetishes and the one you'll be trained and controlled in. The second one is financial fetish / domination as in a fetish based bill paying cash piggy.

As I train you and command how and what to eat force you to gain weight and become disgustingly fat and lazy for me, you will pay for a fraction of my weekly grocery bill. Every week you will see a Forced Feeding Cash Pig pay to view popping up for you to buy and follow. The pay to view fee is the financial draining part (so higher than a usual pay to view which surmounts to 50% of my weekly grocery bill). Inside of each pay to view you will be given a detailed daily eating plan for a seven day consecutive duration! This is a generalized forced feeding (forced to gain weight/ forced to eat) plan and will not be adjusted for your allergies and food preferences. If you would prefer personal attention and be given a customized to you forced feeding diet and training plan you may request this via my "EAT, GAIN WEIGHT & PAY YOUR DUES" fetish training contract. You can find this Contract at http://goddessbelladonnasstore.com in the fetish training contract category section.

Now let's begin with this first one in the generalized forced feeding, forced to gain weight / forced to eat plan. From the moment you eat your Breakfast which you will do within 30 minutes of getting up you will eat the next snack or meal on the list every 2 hours if you are hungry or not. You are forbidden to exercise for the first 6 weeks of beginning this pay to view Forced Feeding Cash Pig generalized training in order to assure you don't counteract the weight gain I am forcing your body into. After the 7th week you will be able work out a little bit under my orders to at least keep your heart strong enough to carry the extra fat your arteries will be building up.

Day #1

Breakfast: 3 scrambled Eggs fried in butter and seasoned with salt and pepper. 4 slices of Bacon and 1 cup of brown sugar cream of wheat. 2 X 8 ounces of Vitamin D Milk and one glass of Orange Juice.

Snack: One big piece of NY Cheesecake with one cup of strawberries (cut up and sugared) plus Vanilla Milkshake

Lunch: 16 oz Steak fried up with onions. One fully loaded (butter, sour cream and cheddar cheese) baked Potatoes. 1 large Garden Salad with Buttermilk Ranch Dressings with shredded cheddar and croutons. 2 Cans of your favorite full flavor Soda.

Snack: One cup of chocolate pudding, 2 Sugar Cookies and 2 cups of Milk.

Dinner: Four pieces of Fried Chicken (2 thighs, 1 Breast and 1 leg). One cup of Cream Corn and one cup of mashed potatoes. One bowl of vanilla Ice-cream. One glass of Vitamin D and 2 cans of full flavored soda.

Snack: 10 Pieces of double stuffed Oreos and 2 bananas. 2 glasses of water and one glass of milk.

Day 2:

Breakfast: 4 envelops of instant oatmeal (Apple and Cinnamon) made with milk with one table spoon of sugar over the top. One cup of coffee with 2 table spoons of sugar and some coffee creamer. One glass of Apple Juice.

Snack: 2 Apple Fritters and 2 cups of Milk

Lunch: A big bowl of hearty beef and vegetable stew (or one Family sized can of premade stew), two slices of garlic bread and one medium sized garden salad with French Dressing. One piece of chocolate cake (triple layer). One chocolate milkshake and 2 cans of full flavored soda.

Snack: 2 Strawberry Shortcakes with lots of whipped cream. One strawberry milkshake

Dinner: Two Big Mac Cheeseburger (or equivalent), two supersized servings of French Fries and 2 big glasses of Iced Tea

Snack: 2 Bananas and one glass of milk

Day 3:

Breakfast: 3 bowls of cereal with sliced fruit. 2 pieces of white toast. One hard boiled Egg. 2 big glasses of milk and one big cup of coffee with 2 table spoons of sugar and coffee creamer.

Snack: One big piece of carrot cake and one can of soda

Lunch: 3 slices of extra cheese with one additional topping of your choice pizza. 10 chicken wings and one serving of French Fries. 3 cans of soda

Snack: One cup of grapes, one large apple and 30 chocolate covered almonds. 2 bottles of water.

Dinner: 6 Fishsticks with tartar sauce. One cup pasta smothered in melted butter and Parmesan Cheese. One salad (small) with thousand Island dressing. 1 soda and one Glass of lemonade.

Snack: 2 large chocolate chip cookies and one big glass of milk.

Day 4:

Breakfast: One full stack of Pancakes (6 Pancakes) smothered with butter, maple syrup, and whipped cream. 2 fried eggs and ½ cup of shredded fried potatoes. 2 glasses of orange juice and one glass of milk.

Snack: One Banana and 10 pieces of vanilla wafers. One chocolate chip milkshake.

Lunch: 10 oz. of either baked Salmon or Catfish. Two cups of white rice with broccoli and cheese sauce. One big Salad with Buttermilk Ranch Dressing. 1 beer or glass of red wine (if you drink) or 2 cans of soda.

Snack: 2 candy bars King sized

Dinner: Two Bratwursts, fried potatoes (3 cut up) and onion, with a Caesar Salad. 2 Cans of Soda.

Snack: One bowl of vanilla Ice-Cream with 2 Snickerdoodles (cookies)

Day 5

Breakfast: French Toast with syrup, 2 scrambled eggs and one serving of hashbrowns. 1 cup of mixed fruit and 2 slices of bacon. One cup of coffee, one glass of orange juice and one glass of milk.

Snack: One triple thick vanilla milkshake and one Banana

Lunch: 3 double cheeseburger and a small French Fries. One large glass of Iced Tea

Snack: One Peanut Butter and Jelly Sandwich with one large glass of Milk

Dinner: Chicken Sandwich (Chicken Filet, 3 leaves of Lettuce, 1 table spoon of Mayo or Miracle Whip, 2 slices of Tomatoes, 2 pieces of Cheese, on white bread). One big bowl of vanilla pudding. One cup of Potato Chips. 2 Cans of Soda

Snack: One piece of Lemon Meringue Pie, one glass of milk

Day 6

Breakfast: 4 pieces of bacon, 2 sausages, 2 fried eggs, 2 pieces of toast, one bowl of Oatmeal plain. One glass of Orange Juice and large glass of milk

Snack: 2 pieces of turtle fudge with one chocolate milkshake

Lunch: 1 Big Mac, one supersized French Fried, one Strawberry Milkshake

Snack: Two Chocolate Chip Cookies and one large glass of milk

Dinner: Two pieces of Fried Chicken, 2 cups of Coleslaw, one large servings French Fries. Two cans of Soda

Snack: Large bowl of Pistachio Pudding with whip cream

Day 7

Breakfast: Four Pecan Pancakes with whipped cream, two fried eggs over easy, one cup of mixed fruit. Two glasses of milk

Snack: 1 Banana and one Peanut Butter and Jelly Sandwich

Lunch: One Steak with fried potatoes with onions. One bowl of green beans.

Snack: Two Oranges and one glass of water

Dinner: Three Porkloin Chops smothered in Mushroom Cream Sauce (see recipe below) with mashed potatoes and 2 pieces of corn on the cob. One glass of red wine or one bottle of beer (if you drink) or 2 Cans of Soda (if you don't).

Snack: One large piece of white cake with chocolate frosting and filling. One glass of milk

Recipe:

Porkloin Chops smothered in Mushroom Cream Sauce

3 thick cut porkloin chops
1 family sized can of Cream of Mushroom Soup (Campbells)
1 package of Onion Soup (Lipton)
1 small package of heavy whipping cream

3 table spoon of flour

Mix together the can of mushroom soup, the package of onion soup, and the package of heavy whipping cream in a pot. Submerge the porkloin chops in the cream soup mixture. Cook on low heat for about 1 hour. Stir frequently.

Check if porkchops are well done. If they are, put them on a plate. Mix the 3 table spoons of flour with a little bit of cold water into a smooth paste. Add the flour mixture into the cream sauce mixture until it thickens. Make sure it doesn't burn. Pour over the porkchops.

If you would like to start being my little forced eating and grocery piggy slave send me a $100 Amazon.com E-Certificate for this weeks orders published here to GoddessBellaDonna@cox.net and contact me to make weekly tribute arrangements for following weekly orders. Weekly cash tribute requirement is $100 cash or $150 E-Certificate.

www.ingramcontent.com/pod-product-compliance
Ingram Content Group UK Ltd.
Pitfield, Milton Keynes, MK11 3LW, UK
UKHW051133260726
13967UKWH00010B/3028